TRIALS
God's Refining Fire

JUNE HUNT

ROSE PUBLISHING/ASPIRE PRESS

Torrance, California

ROSE PUBLISHING/ASPIRE PRESS

Trials: God's Refining Fire
Copyright © 2015 Hope For The Heart
All rights reserved.
Aspire Press, a division of Rose Publishing, Inc.
4733 Torrance Blvd., #259
Torrance, California 90503 USA
www.aspirepress.com

Register your book at www.aspirepress.com/register
Get inspiration via email, sign up at www.aspirepress.com

The information and solutions offered in this resource are a result of years of Bible study, research, and practical life application. They are intended as guidelines for healthy living and are not a replacement for professional medical advice and counseling. JUNE HUNT and HOPE FOR THE HEART make no warranties, representations, or guarantees regarding any particular result or outcome. Any and all express or implied warranties are disclaimed. Please consult qualified medical, pastoral, and psychological professionals regarding individual conditions and needs. JUNE HUNT and HOPE FOR THE HEART do not advocate that you treat yourself or someone you know and disclaim any and all liability arising directly or indirectly from the information in this resource. For more information on Hope For The Heart, visit www.hopefortheheart.org or call 1-800-488-HOPE (4673).

Printed in the United States of America
020615RRD

CONTENTS

Dear Friend,

Because of trials encountered early in my life, I grew up knowing resentment as well as most people know their best friend. In fact, for years I didn't have a best friend. Fearful of inviting an outsider into my private pain, I directed my energy not toward friendships, but toward *justifying* seething hatred of an individual I viewed as Personal Enemy #1: my father.

The mental list I kept of my father's perceived sins and shortcomings was nearly endless: abusive, arrogant, angry, amoral, and that was just for starters. Though I didn't know it at the time, presiding as the virtual judge and jury over his life was a burden I was neither *designed* nor *equipped* to bear. As a result, my ever-expanding list—along with my certainty that dad would never change—gradually ripped the hope right out of my heart.

So much so that, on a hot summer day shortly before starting my junior year in high school, I remember thinking these exact words: "Do it, June! Drive off the bridge! It would be so easy! Why not?" As a newly licensed driver, I gripped the steering wheel of my car and seriously considered whether this would be the day to bring a quick and welcome end to a life of just 15 years.

With my foot poised on the accelerator and the compulsion to press down growing, suddenly I felt an overpowering restraint. "Wait! What if I'm not successful? I could end up only maiming myself. Then Mom (whom I adored) would have the huge burden of needing to take care of me the rest of my life!"

How vividly I remember the painful emotions churning inside of me and the hopelessness that ushered such upheaval into my life. It wasn't that I *wanted* to kill myself; I just wanted to stop the pain—relentless, unspoken, soul-ravaging pain—produced by a fiery trial that seemed to have no end.

What would have happened during the apex of that trial had I ignored my inner voice of restraint and, instead, careened over the expressway bridge? With the benefit of hindsight, I invite you to pause with me now to consider: Would I have been alive to accept Christ the following year … as I did? Would I have experienced the awesome privilege of leading my father to a saving faith in Christ six months before he succumbed to cancer … as I did? Would I have been available for God to use me to found a worldwide ministry that, today, brings *biblical hope and practical help* worldwide … as He has?

I'll never know the answers to these questions on this side of heaven, but I do know this: Had I not persevered during the trials in my life, I would have no personal testimony of God's faithfulness, no ironclad assurance of His ability to rescue and restore.

You see, in both the Old and New Testaments, we find numerous references to our God refining us through painful trials in much the same way an earthly refiner uses fire to purify gold and silver. God's purpose for this process is *to conform our character to His.*

Clearly, we don't develop Christlike character all at once. It's forged over time, especially through *trials*. Helping you hang on to hope in the midst of these trials—especially when the heat is turned up beyond what you think you can bear—is why I wrote this book. Page by page, it provides *biblical hope and practical help* so you can draw near to the heart of the One who allowed the trial, trust in His perfect plan and character, and confidently surrender your will to His will.

As you do, you can have utmost assurance that the *"momentary affliction"* (2 Corinthians 4:17 ESV) God allows in your life is immensely purposeful. The heat will not destroy you, only conform you to Christ's character. You can rest in the timeless truth of Isaiah 43:2: *"When you pass through the waters, I will be with you; and when you pass through the rivers, they will not sweep over you. When you walk through the fire, you will not be burned; the flames will not set you ablaze."*

In my own life, the facts are clear: God, through His matchless mercy and grace, turned my own personal *mess* into a *message*. He transformed my *test* into a *testimony*. And friend, you can be sure of this: If He did it for me, He can do it for you—for your gladness and His great glory!

Yours in the Lord's hope,

June Hunt

TRIALS
God's Refining Fire

Everyone undergoes change in a crucible.

Everyone faces the heat in a furnace.

Everyone can be refined by the Refiner.

This is the pursuit of our personal Refiner—to purify us. And He is masterful at knowing how much heat is needed and how much time it takes in the Refiner's fire to surface impurities in our character. Whether refining precious metals or refining precious people, one point is certain: Purity is *never* achieved from only one firing in the furnace.

Just like a silversmith or a goldsmith, God is determined to delete the dross from our lives so that we'll shine as He intends. It is the image of Christ He wants clearly reflected in our lives. The refining process begins on this side of heaven and is finally finished on the other.

Meanwhile, Scripture encourages us ...

> "And we all, who with unveiled faces contemplate the Lord's glory, are being transformed into his image with ever-increasing glory, which comes from the Lord, who is the Spirit."
> (2 Corinthians 3:18)

DEFINITIONS

Every one of us faces testing trials and fiery trials at different times. When they occur, we often wonder, "Why *this*?" "Why *now*?" "Why *me*?"

The next time you feel you are being tested remember what the Bible says in 1 Chronicles 29:17 ...

> "I know, my God,
> that you test the heart
> and are pleased with integrity."

Think about the role of a silversmith. A silversmith is in the business of separation—removing the unwanted impurities from the silver to achieve the highest degree of purity possible. This would be an impossible task without *heat*.

Impurities are released only when the temperature is turned "way up." The same is true when we have deeply embedded flaws and defects in our character. These are surfaced only by the fiery heat *of trials and testings*.

Incredible change occurs in the crucible.

A crucible is a pot made of clay, porcelain, or iron that is capable of sustaining extremely high temperatures. Silversmiths of old, those you would find bartering and bargaining in the corner markets of ancient Jerusalem, would grind up chunks of crude silver, place the granular material in a crucible, and then place the crucible in a furnace over an open fire.

The silversmith would watch and wait, keeping an eye on the furnace, continually evaluating temperature as well as time in the blazing heat. Totally attentive, his concern is the crucible, cognizant that a tremendous transformation is in the making.

A curious substance begins to form on the surface of the now molten metal, a scummy layer of material that the silversmith is eager to slough off and remove—forever. The useless impurities have no redeeming value in silver, *nor in our lives.*

When our "dross" is removed, then God transforms us into something both beautiful and useful.

> "He has made everything
> beautiful in its time."
> (Ecclesiastes 3:11)

▶ **Trials** are the process of proving the quality or worth of something or someone.[1]

▶ **Trials** are tests of your faith, patience, or endurance through the process of suffering.[2]

▶ **"Trials"** in Greek is primarily three different words, each with a slightly different meaning, yet all reveal God's purpose for trials and suffering.[3]

- *Dokimion*: proven faith

  A testing trial proves whether or not your faith is genuine.

  "In all this you greatly rejoice, though now for a little while you may have had to suffer grief in all kinds of trials. These have come so that the proven genuineness of your faith—of greater worth than gold, which perishes even though refined by fire—may result in praise, glory and honor when Jesus Christ is revealed" (1 Peter 1:6–7).

- *Purosis*: refined character

  A fiery trial refines your character, as gold is refined (implies suffering).

  "Do not be surprised at the fiery trial when it comes upon you to test you, as though something strange were happening to you" (1 Peter 4:12 ESV).

- *Peirasmos:* tested commitment

  A testing trial or temptation determines the quality of your commitment.

  "Consider it pure joy, my brothers and sisters, whenever you face trials of many kinds, because you know that the testing of your faith produces perseverance. Let perseverance finish its work so that you may be mature and complete, not lacking anything" (James 1:2–4).

In the Bible, many references present the refining of gold and silver as a parallel of God's refining us through our own painful trials. This unforgettable allegory is meant to help us understand the purpose behind our pain—specifically, to conform us to the character of Christ.

Clearly, we don't develop Christlike character all at once. Character is forged over time, especially through fiery trials. Indeed, God is our Refiner.

> "For you, God, tested us;
> you refined us like silver."
> (Psalm 66:10)

Because the Bible is filled with images of God working as the Refiner in our lives, we can gain much insight by understanding the refining process.

The Six Stages of Refinement

▶ **STAGE 1: The Breaking**

The refiner breaks up the natural ore.

- In biblical times, a refiner began by breaking up rough ore—hardened rock encased with common minerals (such as tin, copper, and zinc), but which also may possibly contain rare metals, the precious metals of gold and silver.

- Breaking the rock is necessary to begin the refining process of exposing highly valuable metals to heat.

- The Lord states, *"My people* [are] *the ore"* (Jeremiah 6:27). We are rough rock in need of hammering, breaking, and refining.

> "'Is not my word like fire,'
> declares the LORD,
> 'and like a hammer that breaks
> a rock in pieces?'"
> (Jeremiah 23:29)

▶ **STAGE 2: The Crucible**

The refiner places unrefined silver or gold into a crucible.

- The refiner puts broken, crushed ore into a crucible—a fireproof melting pot able to withstand intense heat.

- Then the refiner places the crucible into the furnace at the precise temperature necessary for separating out inferior metals that would otherwise mar the quality of the gold or silver.

- Just as the furnace is used to purify silver in the crucible, our Refiner uses the heat of a severe test or a life-impacting trial to purify our hearts and cleanse our character.

"The crucible for silver and the furnace for gold, but the Lord tests the heart."
(Proverbs 17:3)

▶ STAGE 3: The Dross

The refiner places the crucible in the heated furnace to remove dross.

- As the ore melts in the crucible under the watchful eye of the refiner, a layer of impurities, called dross, eventually appears. (Dross refers to the scum that forms on the surface of the liquefied molten metal.)

"Remove the dross from the silver, and a silversmith can produce a vessel."
(Proverbs 25:4)

- For us individually, dross represents anything impure or worthless—any wrong motive, wrong attitude, wrong action—any sin that keeps us from being all God created us to be. Yet, the Word of God states the problem succinctly: *"Your silver has become dross"* (Isaiah 1:22).

▶ STAGE 4: The Heat

The refiner raises the temperature to higher degrees.

- The heat extracts the dross—the impurities emitted during the refining process. After the refiner painstakingly skims off these impurities, he then increases the heat and places the crucible back into the blistering furnace.

- Again and again (up to seven times, we are told in historical literature) impurities rise to the surface. Again and again, the crucible is returned to the furnace.

- Our Refiner knows the exact temperature needed to extract the dross, and He knows that only certain impurities are released at certain temperatures. How interesting that Psalm 12:6 says ...

"And the words of the LORD are flawless,
like silver purified in a crucible,
like gold refined seven times."

▶ STAGE 5: The Purification

The refiner continues to remove the impurities.

- Each time, with utmost skill and patience, the refiner removes layer after layer of dross and increasingly, the silver and gold become more pure and precious than before.

- To gauge his progress, the refiner looks for his own reflection on the surface of the crucible's contents. The more dross removed, the less distorted his reflection.

- Notice, the refiner never leaves the crucible—he sits by it. The Bible says our Refiner sits over the refining process to purify us.

> "He will sit as a refiner and purifier of silver; he will purify ... and refine them like gold and silver."
> (Malachi 3:3)

▶ STAGE 6: The Reflection

The refiner sees a clear image of himself.

- Initially, the refiner looks into the pot and sees a dim reflection of himself.

- Only after repeatedly skimming off the top layer of dross floating on the surface, and only when the refiner looks into the metal-filled crucible and sees a clear reflection of himself is the process complete. Finally, the metal attains its highest degree of purity!

- And that describes our Refiner's loving intentions for allowing us to be in the "*furnace of affliction.*" As we trust Him to use our trials to cleanse our character and purify our hearts, we will begin to see the "silver lining."

"See, I have refined you,
though not as silver; I have tested
you in the furnace of affliction."
(Isaiah 48:10)

When it comes to trials, without a doubt, some are "hotter" than others.

The Master Refiner can use the loss of a job or the loss of a loved one to surface dross in our character, or He can fulfill His divine purposes through the pain of a rocky relationship or a menacing medical diagnosis. Certain impurities will rise to the top—*only with utmost heat.*

And like refiners of silver, who slough off that slimy layer of waste in the crucible, God sloughs off the impurities in our lives. What follows next is a fascinating step. Silversmiths peer into their crucibles, eyes squinting to scrutinize the surface of the molten metals, searching for an image—*their very own image.* If what stares back at them is cloudy and dull, the crucible is placed back into the sweltering inferno for further purification.

Likewise, our Master Refiner is committed to completion.

"Being confident of this, that he who began a good work in you will carry it on to completion until the day of Christ Jesus." (Philippians 1:6)

▶ **Trials** are experienced by everyone.

"Everyone who wants to live a godly life in Christ Jesus will be persecuted" (2 Timothy 3:12).

▶ **Trials** have a divine purpose.

"Not only so, but we also glory in our sufferings, because we know that suffering produces perseverance; perseverance, character; and character, hope. And hope does not put us to shame" (Romans 5:3–5).

▶ **Trials** last only for a while.

"For our light and momentary troubles are achieving for us an eternal glory that far outweighs them all" (2 Corinthians 4:17).

▶ **Trials** are controlled by God.

"God ... will not let you be tempted beyond what you can bear" (1 Corinthians 10:13).

▶ **Trials** come with God's grace for endurance.

"My grace is sufficient for you, for my power is made perfect in weakness" (2 Corinthians 12:9).

▶ **Trials** strengthen you in your weaknesses.

"I delight in weaknesses, in insults, in hardships, in persecutions, in difficulties. For when I am weak, then I am strong" (2 Corinthians 12:10).

Purification is a painstaking process.

The choicest silver or gold—*like the choicest character*—undergoes the Refiner's fire numerous times to attain the highest degree of purity possible. When silversmiths or goldsmiths finally saw a perfectly clear image of themselves in the crucible, they knew purification had been achieved.

In 1874, Emil Wohlwill invented a refining process for gold that today produces the purest precious metal possible—99.999%.[4] But when God finishes refining His people, there will not be even a speck of imperfection. The uncompromising goal—*100%*—will be attained to radiate the perfection of Christ Himself.

Facing the agony of the cross, Jesus was in great physical, mental, emotional, and spiritual distress, to the point of beseeching the Father three times whether there might be another way to redeem us, but there was none.

Jesus faced the last and most painful trip to the crucible of God's refining fire, not out of weakness and defeat but out of strength and faith in the Father, who loved Him. Jesus was able to trust the Father's trial because He trusted the Father's heart of love and compassion, wisdom and understanding. And you can face the trials He has designed for you because He has the same love for you that He has for Jesus.

"I have given them the glory
that you gave me,
that they may be one as we are one—
I in them and you in me—
so that they may be brought
to complete unity.
Then the world will know that you sent me
and have loved them
even as you have loved me."
(John 17:22–23)

God's Heart on Trials

▶ **God desires** to use trials to produce in you a heart of humility that He might honor you.

"Humble yourselves, therefore, under God's mighty hand, that he may lift you up in due time" (1 Peter 5:6).

▶ **God plans** to use trials to lead you to a point of personal examination that He might set you on a correction course.

"Search me, God, and know my heart; test me and know my anxious thoughts. See if there is any offensive way in me, and lead me in the way everlasting" (Psalm 139:23–24).

▶ **God designs** trials to direct you to Him that He might reveal His ways to you.

"It was good for me to be afflicted so that I might learn your decrees" (Psalm 119:71).

▶ **God develops** trials to keep you dependent on His Word that He might teach you obedience.

"Before I was afflicted I went astray, but now I obey your word" (Psalm 119:67).

▶ **God depends** on trials to drive you to pour out your heart to Him that He might extend mercy to you.

"I cry aloud to the LORD; I lift up my voice to the LORD for mercy. I pour out before him my complaint; before him I tell my trouble. When my spirit grows faint within me, it is you who watch over my way" (Psalm 142:1–3).

▶ **God utilizes** trials to reveal your sinfulness that in love He might break the power of sin in your life.

"Surely it was for my benefit that I suffered such anguish. In your love you kept me from the pit of destruction; you have put all my sins behind your back" (Isaiah 38:17).

▶ **God sees** trials as a motivation for you to reach out to Him that He might compassionately listen to you and encourage you.

"You, LORD, hear the desire of the afflicted; you encourage them, and you listen to their cry" (Psalm 10:17).

▶ **God employs** trials to expose wrongful thinking that He might bring you to the truth and cause you to rejoice in Him.

"As the deer pants for streams of water, so
my soul pants for you, my God.
My soul thirsts for God, for the living God.
When can I go and meet with God?
My tears have been my food day and night,
while people say to me all day long,
'Where is your God?' These things I
remember as I pour out my soul:
how I used to go to the house of God under
the protection of the Mighty One
with shouts of joy and praise
among the festive throng.
Why, my soul, are you downcast?
Why so disturbed within me?
Put your hope in God, for I will yet praise
him, my Savior and my God."
(Psalm 42:1–5)

CHARACTERISTICS

When it comes to trials, theirs could not be more traumatic.

When it comes to degrees of suffering, theirs could not be more sweltering.

Tremendous tragedy befalls a man beloved by God, *"the greatest man among all the people of the East"* (Job 1:3). In order to test his highly esteemed servant, God allows Satan to wreak havoc in Job's life, stripping him of all his wealth, killing his ten children, and inflicting him with painful sores from head to toe. Job and his wife have different reactions to God, the Master Refiner, who allows such suffering in their lives and has seemingly walked away.

Both Job and his wife suffer greatly and are laid low by their severe trial, but the truth of Scripture eventually will be fulfilled in Job's life.

> "He knows the way that I take;
> when he has tested me,
> I will come forth as gold."
> (Job 23:10)

It's a startling scene, impossible to stomach—a plummet from prolific prosperity to prolific pain—too hard, too severe to bear.

Her husband once garnered the respect of the entire community, taking his seat in the city square among the noblest and wisest of men. The younger ones would step aside in honor. The older rose to their feet eager to greet the man both highly esteemed and highly blessed of God.

But now the memory seems like a dream, the vision of grandeur *vanished*. For now, Job sits in an ash heap scraping himself with a broken piece of pottery. He has been pummeled by Satan with painful sores all over his body, and Job's wife finds words welling up in her spirit that wail with the bitter agony of a gravely wounded heart. She reels with resentment that she and Job are still captives inside the crucible with the blistering flame beneath them.

Addressing Job, she verbally lashes out: *"Are you still maintaining your integrity? Curse God and die!"* (Job 2:9).

The following acrostic indeed summarizes the intensity of these **TRIALS**.

T —Temporary Troubles

▪ Loss of possessions

"One day ... a messenger came to Job and said, 'The oxen were plowing and the donkeys were grazing nearby, and the Sabeans attacked and made off with them...' While he was still speaking, another messenger came and said, 'The fire of God fell from the heavens and burned up the sheep and the servants ...' While he was still speaking, another messenger came and said, 'The Chaldeans formed three raiding parties and swept down on your camels and made off with them'" (Job 1:13–17).

▪ Loss of security

"Surely, God, you have worn me out; you have devastated my entire household. You have shriveled me up—and it has become a witness; my gauntness rises up and testifies against me" (Job 16:7–8).

R —Relational Ruptures

- **Loss of reputation**

  "I have become a laughingstock to my friends ... a mere laughingstock, though righteous and blameless!" (Job 12:4).

- **Loss of acceptance and trust**

  "Oh, for the days when I was in my prime, when God's intimate friendship blessed my house, when the Almighty was still with me and my children were around me" (Job 29:4–5).

I —Inexplicable Injustices

- **Loss of understanding**

  "Does God pervert justice? Does the Almighty pervert what is right?" (Job 8:3).

- **Loss of insight**

  "Even if I washed myself with soap and my hands with cleansing powder, you would plunge me into a slime pit so that even my clothes would detest me" (Job 9:30–31).

A —All-Consuming Affliction

- **Loss of health**

So Satan went out from the presence of the LORD and afflicted Job with painful sores from the soles of his feet to the crown of his head. Then Job took a piece of broken pottery and scraped himself with it as he sat among the ashes" (Job 2:7–8).

- **Loss of stability**

"Terrors overwhelm me; my dignity is driven away as by the wind, my safety vanishes like a cloud. And now my life ebbs away; days of suffering grip me" (Job 30:15–16).

L —Lingering Lament

- **Loss of loved ones**

"'Your sons and daughters were feasting and drinking wine at the oldest brother's house, when suddenly a mighty wind swept in from the desert and struck the four corners of the house. It collapsed on them and they are dead'" (Job 1:18–19).

- **Loss of long-term dreams and opportunities**

"I loathe my very life; therefore I will give free rein to my complaint and speak out in the bitterness of my soul" (Job 10:1).

S —Spiritual Suffering

▪ Loss of peace

"When I think my bed will comfort me and my couch will ease my complaint, even then you frighten me with dreams and terrify me with visions, so that I prefer strangling and death, rather than this body of mine. I despise my life; I would not live forever. Let me alone; my days have no meaning" (Job 7:13–16).

▪ Loss of purpose

"Why is light given to those in misery, and life to the bitter of soul, to those who long for death that does not come, who search for it more than for hidden treasure?" (Job 3:20–21).

The mere presence of pain is not a promise that dross will be removed from your life. The trial itself does not produce purity. Your attitude and response toward your trial helps determine what God will accomplish in your life.

Do you resist God's grace by bitter murmuring and complaining, or do you respond to your hardship with a humble heart, surrendering to the sovereign hand that controls the crucible?

> "Humble yourselves, therefore,
> under God's mighty hand,
> that he may lift you up in due time."
> (1 Peter 5:6)

▶ HARDENED HEART

"God doesn't care about me—my suffering will never end."

HUMBLE HEART

"My suffering had a beginning and it will also have an ending."

"The God of all grace, who called you to his eternal glory in Christ, after you have suffered a little while, will himself restore you and make you strong, firm and steadfast" (1 Peter 5:10).

▶ HARDENED HEART

"It's not fair —no one is suffering like me."

HUMBLE HEART

"I am no different than others. God allows all His children to suffer."

"You know that the family of believers throughout the world is undergoing the same kind of sufferings" (1 Peter 5:9).

▶ HARDENED HEART

"The Lord turned His back on me—and left me broken."

HUMBLE HEART

"God is especially close to me when my heart is broken."

"The LORD is close to the brokenhearted and saves those who are crushed in spirit" (Psalm 34:18).

▶ HARDENED HEART

"I've had too many troubles. Life is cruel—so is God."

HUMBLE HEART

"I will accept both bad and good in life because God is sovereign over it all."

"Shall we accept good from God, and not trouble?" (Job 2:10).

▶ Hardened Heart

"I cried out to God—but He didn't hear me."

Humble Heart

"God cares about my suffering, and He hears my cry for help."

"He has not despised or scorned the suffering of the afflicted one; he has not hidden his face from him but has listened to his cry for help" (Psalm 22:24).

▶ Hardened Heart

"Faith doesn't work—I had it, yet still suffered."

Humble Heart

"Faith does not prevent suffering. Actually, the godly are called to suffer."

"It has been granted to you on behalf of Christ not only to believe in him, but also to suffer for him" (Philippians 1:29).

►Hardened Heart

"I'll never turn to God—He would never help me!"

Humble Heart

"I can approach God about anything. I'm confident He will help me."

"Let us then approach God's throne of grace with confidence, so that we may receive mercy and find grace to help us in our time of need" (Hebrews 4:16).

►Hardened Heart

"God has failed me by not removing this suffering."

Humble Heart

"Although God allows this suffering, He will speak to me during it and ultimately deliver me."

"Those who suffer he delivers in their suffering; he speaks to them in their affliction" (Job 36:15).

Suffering and Sin

QUESTION: "Aren't all trials and suffering the result of sin?"

ANSWER: Sometimes yes, sometimes no. In some situations, suffering can be the direct result of a person's destructive choice.

In other cases, God often allows the innocent to suffer in order to display His power and divine purposes.

"His disciples asked him,
'Rabbi, who sinned, this man or his parents,
that he was born blind?'
'Neither this man nor his parents sinned,'
said Jesus, 'but this happened [he was born
blind] so that the works of God
might be displayed in him.'"
(John 9:2–3)

Job and his wife both suffer from broken hearts. When one calamity after another befalls their family, it feels like blustery bellows fanning the flame. This husband and wife respond to their tragic trials in drastically different ways—while Job sits among the ashes scraping his sores, his wife cries out in hopeless agony and despair. Thus a battle against the bellows ensues, a fight against the flames of the crucible.

"You are talking like a foolish woman. Shall we accept good from God, and not trouble?" (Job 2:10). Her answer would seem to be a resounding NO! Gone are all her children. Once prosperous, she is now penniless; once the proud wife of a man sitting in a judge's chair, she is now the bitter wife of a man reduced to sitting in sackcloth and ashes.

Job's wife perceives God's crucible as an instrument to singe her faith rather than strengthen it, preventing her from seeing past her present devastation to a future filled with hope. Truly, focus can prove to be everything!

But while the Master Refiner seems absent, in truth God's ears hear every conversation and His eyes see every event surrounding the traumatic testing. Just like the silversmiths of old, God never once looks away from the fiery crucible. His love keeps Him focused on His cherished treasure.

And what Job's wife may not realize is that the utmost heat is needed when seeking to surface possible impurities in a man God considers *"blameless and upright"* (Job 1:1). And what Job's wife can't even begin to imagine is that double blessing awaits around the corner at the conclusion of the trial.

Even in the darkest of circumstances, Job's story should give us hope.

"The Lord blessed the latter part of Job's life more than the former part."
(Job 42:12)

Fighting the Flames

God has already provided the grace for each of us to be triumphant through the most severe of trials, yet some of us refuse to submit to His sovereign reign over our lives.

Those who fight the flames of the crucible are commonly characterized by:

▶ **Destructive** anger

▶ **Depleted** energy

▶ **Drained** emotions

▶ **Diminished** joy

▶ **Depressed** outlook

▶ **Damaging** accusations

▶ **Decreased** interests

▶ **Deteriorating** self-worth

▶ **Desire** to escape

▶ **Distrust** of others

▶ **Doubt** of God

▶ **Distraction** from priorities

▶ **Dulled** spiritual sensitivity

Facing the Flames

Knowing and accepting the love and purposes of God enables us to submit to His will for our lives and to His sovereign rule over our lives ... especially when it comes to crucibles.

Those who face the flames of the crucible and cooperate with God's purposes keep their focus on the good that will result from them, and thus are commonly characterized by:

▶ **A keener awareness** of God

▶ **An acute realization** that God is always working through all circumstances

▶ **A greater capacity** to discern between good and evil

▶ **An increased ability** to rise above daily stress

▶ **A positive outlook** when trouble comes

▶ **A deeper understanding** of the ways of God and others

▶ **A biblical viewpoint** for making difficult decisions

▶ **A sincere heart** for the heavenly calling

▶ **An optimistic attitude** toward life

▶ **A firmer faith** in the goodness of God

▶ **A deeper, more intimate relationship** with God

▶ **An abiding joy** and sense of peace

▶ **A growing sense** of having value, of being loved, significant, and secure

> **"Press on toward the goal to win the prize for which God has called [you] heavenward in Christ Jesus."**
> **(Philippians 3:14)**

CAUSES

Daniel is an exile with an excruciating trial ahead of him.

He is described as a young man of exceptional character *"without any physical defect, handsome, showing aptitude for every kind of learning, well informed, quick to understand, and qualified to serve in the king's palace"* (Daniel 1:4).

His cherished homeland is war-torn, and his beloved city, Jerusalem, has been besieged by the powerful king Nebuchadnezzar. In the end, Daniel is hauled off to Babylon to begin three years of strict training for service in the royal courts of the reviled king.

After supernaturally interpreting an astounding dream, he quickly gains favor in the king's eyes and rises to prominence as ruler over the entire province. Daniel's stellar leadership qualities and integrity are duly noted by a subsequent king, Darius, who intends to put Daniel in charge of his entire kingdom!

Interestingly, commendation comes from two kings, but *condemnation* then comes from his colleagues. *"Now Daniel so distinguished himself among the administrators and the satraps by his exceptional qualities that the king planned to set him over the whole kingdom. At this, the administrators and the satraps tried to find grounds for charges against Daniel in his conduct of government affairs, but they were unable to do so"* (Daniel 6:3–4).

WHAT CALLS Us to the Crucible?

God not only calls Daniel to commitment and to be courageous, He calls him to endure the crucible while malicious whispers become malevolent roars by those seeking his demise.

Daniel's envious colleagues pursue evidence of wrongdoing on his part, but they ...

"... could find no corruption in him, because he was trustworthy and neither corrupt nor negligent. Finally these men said,
'We will never find any basis for charges against this man Daniel unless it has something to do with the law of his God.'"
(Daniel 6:4–5)

So they manipulate King Darius to issue an edict, one that undoubtedly appeals to his pride.

The royal decree for the next 30 days proclaims that anyone who prays to anyone other than the king will be thrown into the lions' den.

However, Daniel's devotion to God involves daily prayer and a disciplined life.

> **"Three times a day he got down on his knees and prayed, giving thanks to his God, just as he had done before.**
> **Then these men went as a group and found Daniel praying and asking God for help."**
> **(Daniel 6:10–11)**

Like Daniel, God has called you to be a person not just of exceptional character, but of Christlike character—of godly character. And like Daniel, He will take you into and through various trials to develop that precious, pristine character in you.

Called to Be in the Crucible

▶ **You are called to be committed.**

- God calls you to endure the pain of unjust suffering because of your commitment to follow Christ.

- While Scripture is clear that every authentic Christian experiences the Lord's provision, to follow in His footsteps means you will also be called to suffer unjustly.

   "For it is commendable if someone bears up under the pain of unjust suffering because they are conscious of God. But

how is it to your credit if you receive a beating for doing wrong and endure it? But if you suffer for doing good and you endure it, this is commendable before God. To this you were called, because Christ suffered for you, leaving you an example, that you should follow in his steps. 'He committed no sin, and no deceit was found in his mouth.' When they hurled their insults at him, he did not retaliate; when he suffered, he made no threats. Instead, he entrusted himself to him who judges justly" (1 Peter 2:19–23).

▶ **You are called to be corrected.**

- God disciplines you because He loves you— you are His beloved child.

- Self-will may detour you from God's preferred path for your life, and you may suffer consequences for your choices. But your heavenly Father will redirect your steps to put you back on a correction course. That is why the Bible says ...

  "Endure hardship as discipline; God is treating you as his children. For what children are not disciplined by their father?" (Hebrews 12:7)

▶ **You are called to be compassionate.**

- Suffering, however painful, can become the catalyst that gives you a heart of compassion for others.

- During times of trial, your most lasting lessons come from the comfort and counsel of God.

  "Praise be to the God and Father of our Lord Jesus Christ, the Father of compassion and the God of all comfort, who comforts us in all our troubles, so that we can comfort those in any trouble with the comfort we ourselves receive from God. For just as we share abundantly in the sufferings of Christ, so also our comfort abounds through Christ" (2 Corinthians 1:3–5).

▶ **You are called to be courageous.**

- God calls you to take a stand for truth and righteousness in the midst of wrong.

- Those who choose to live godly lives in the midst of ungodly, worldly values will be criticized and persecuted.

  "Everyone who wants to live a godly life in Christ Jesus will be persecuted" (2 Timothy 3:12).

▶ You are called to be a conqueror.

- God allows Satan to tempt and attack you, just as he did with Jesus, in order that you can stand against the enemy and claim victory in Christ's strength.

- Jesus defeated Satan, and you are more than a conqueror in Him.

    "No, in all things we are more than conquerors through him who loved us" (Romans 8:37).

▶ You are called to be Christlike.

- God designs refining fires to surface and cleanse impurities from your character and to conform you to Christ.

- You can accept your fiery trials when you accept God's purifying purpose.

    "For those God foreknew he also predestined to be conformed to the image of his Son" (Romans 8:29).

Love and Suffering

QUESTION: "Does God care about my suffering?"

ANSWER: Know that your Heavenly Father loves you deeply and cares greatly about your suffering as demonstrated by the fact that:

▶ He is close to you when you are brokenhearted.

"The LORD is close to the brokenhearted and saves those who are crushed in spirit" (Psalm 34:18).

▶ He stays around you in the midst of trouble.

"The angel of the LORD encamps around those who fear him, and he delivers them" (Psalm 34:7).

▶ He keeps record of your grief and keeps hold of your tears.

"You have kept count of my tossings; put my tears in your bottle. Are they not in your book?" (Psalm 56:8 ESV).

Scripture lays out various contributing factors that make a trip to God's refining crucible necessary. For those still in the grip of sin's deadly control it is the need for purification from head to toe. Those who have been purified but become contaminated again by sin's deceitful delicacies need to be purged of the dross their deeds have created.

We are all a work in progress, and we can trust our Lord to refine our character. The books of Daniel and Jeremiah lend insight into the need we all have for making repeated trips to God's refining crucible.

▶ Stumbling

"Some of the wise will stumble, so that they may be refined, purified and made spotless until the time of the end, for it will still come at the appointed time" (Daniel 11:35).

▶ Wickedness

"Many will be purified, made spotless and refined, but the wicked will continue to be wicked. None of the wicked will understand, but those who are wise will understand" (Daniel 12:10).

▶ Untested ways

"I have made you a tester of metals and my people the ore, that you may observe and test their ways" (Jeremiah 6:27).

▶ Rebellion

"They are all hardened rebels, going about to slander" (Jeremiah 6:28).

▶ Corruption

"They are bronze and iron; they all act corruptly" (Jeremiah 6:28).

▶ Hardness

"The bellows blow fiercely to burn away the lead with fire" (Jeremiah 6:29).

▶ Unrepentance

"The refining goes on in vain; the wicked are not purged out" (Jeremiah 6:29).

Sadly, those who refuse to be refined in God's crucible, will ultimately reap the result of their choice. They will pay the price that sin demands—they will be rejected by the One they have rejected and they will perish in their sins, unrefined, unpurified, unsaved!

**"They are called rejected silver,
because the Lord has rejected them."
(Jeremiah 6:30)**

The root cause of discontentment in the crucible is disappointment with God's appointment, the denouncement or denial of His sovereign, perfect plan.

But that's *not* the case with Daniel. His colleagues indeed trap him, but he knows *who allows* them to trap him.

Distressed upon hearing the men's report, King Darius tries to find any and every way to rescue Daniel from the ferocious jaws of the lions. But the hastily issued edict proves irrevocable and the king is obligated and duty-bound to punish Daniel.

Daniel is thrown into the lions' lair, prompting the king to exclaim while holding on to hope...

> **"May your God, whom you serve
> continually, rescue you!"
> (Daniel 6:16)**

Three God-Given Inner Needs

In reality, we have all been created with three God-given inner needs: the needs for love, significance, and security.[5]

▶**Love**—to know that someone is unconditionally committed to our best interest

"My command is this: Love each other as I have loved you" (John 15:12).

▶**Significance**—to know that our lives have meaning and purpose

"I cry out to God Most High, to God who fulfills his purpose for me" (Psalm 57:2 ESV).

▶**Security**—to feel accepted and a sense of belonging

"Whoever fears the LORD has a secure
fortress, and for their children
it will be a refuge."
(Proverbs 14:26)

The Ultimate Need-Meeter

Why did God give us these deep inner needs, knowing that people fail people and self-effort fails us as well?

God gave us these inner needs so that we would come to know Him as our Need-Meeter. Our needs are designed by God to draw us into a deeper dependence on Christ. God did not create any person or position or any amount of power or possessions to meet the deepest needs in our lives. If a person or thing *could* meet all our needs, we wouldn't need God! The Lord will use circumstances and bring positive people into our lives as an extension of His care and compassion, but ultimately only God can satisfy all the needs of our hearts.

The Bible says ...

> "The LORD will guide you always; he will satisfy your needs in a sun-scorched land and will strengthen your frame. You will be like a well-watered garden, like a spring whose waters never fail." (Isaiah 58:11)

The apostle Paul revealed this truth by first asking, *"What a wretched man I am! Who will rescue me from this body that is subject to death?"* and then by answering his own question in saying it is *"Jesus Christ our Lord!"* (Romans 7:24–25).

All along, the Lord planned to meet our deepest needs for ...

▶ **Love**—*"I* [the Lord] *have loved you with an everlasting love; I have drawn you with unfailing kindness"* (Jeremiah 31:3).

▶ **Significance**—*"'For I know the plans I have for you,' declares the Lord, 'plans to prosper you and not to harm you, plans to give you hope and a future'"* (Jeremiah 29:11).

▶ **Security**—*"The Lord himself goes before you and will be with you; he will never leave you nor forsake you. Do not be afraid; do not be discouraged"* (Deuteronomy 31:8).

The truth is that our God-given needs for love, significance, and security can be legitimately met in Christ Jesus!

Philippians 4:19 makes it plain ...

> **"My God will meet all your needs according to the riches of his glory in Christ Jesus."**

Trials can be the disappointments we experience that are designed to reveal our prideful hearts. Like gold in the crucible, the hotter the fire, the more our imperfections rise to the top.

▶ WRONG BELIEF

"Life is not fair! I don't deserve this much heartache and disappointment."

RIGHT BELIEF

"There are no 'accidents' in life. Since God is sovereign over every situation in my life, I will see my disappointment as God's appointment to build Christlike character in me. I know that at the end of this temporary trial, I will emerge as purified gold."

"But he knows the way that I take; when he has tested me, I will come forth as gold. My feet have closely followed his steps; I have kept to his way without turning aside. I have not departed from the commands of his lips; I have treasured the words of his mouth more than my daily bread" (Job 23:10–12).

In the midst of his anguish, while fretting over the fate of Daniel, the heart of a king is being purified by God.

After ordering Daniel to be thrown into the lions' den, King Darius doesn't eat, doesn't summon his customary evening entertainment, and he doesn't sleep.

King Darius eagerly awaits the light of dawn to see if the God of Daniel has indeed rescued him from the lions, and relief floods his soul upon hearing his servant's voice.

"May the king live forever! My God sent his angel, and he shut the mouths of the lions. They have not hurt me, because I was found innocent in his sight. Nor have I done any wrong before you, Your Majesty" (Daniel 6:21–22).

King Darius is overjoyed, and he issues a far wiser edict that manifests a heart full of faith in the God of Daniel.

"I issue a decree that in every part of my kingdom people must fear and reverence the God of Daniel. 'For he is the living God and he endures forever; his kingdom will not be destroyed, his dominion will never end.

> He rescues and he saves;
> he performs signs and wonders in the
> heavens and on the earth.
> He has rescued Daniel from
> the power of the lions.'"
> (Daniel 6:26–27)

It is always God's heart to rescue, to save, especially those who are still living under the rule and reign of sin. And it is also God's heart to test and refine His people, those He loves, those Jesus died to save.

> "See, I will refine and test them,
> for what else can I do
> because of the sin of my people?"
> (Jeremiah 9:7)

Do you want to move from a "wrong belief" to a "right belief" concerning the trials of life?

Are you longing for assurance that God is truly with you, moving you toward greater conformity to the image of His Son, as well as greater peace and joy?

God has a plan, and it is laid out in the following four points.

Four Points of God's Plan

#1 God's Purpose for You is *Salvation*.

What was God's motivation in sending Jesus Christ to earth?

To express His love for you by saving you!

The Bible says, *"God so loved the world that he gave his one and only Son, that whoever believes in him shall not perish but have eternal life. For God did not send his Son into the world to condemn the world, but to save the world through him"* (John 3:16–17).

What was Jesus' purpose in coming to earth?

To forgive your sins, to empower you to have victory over sin, and to enable you to live a fulfilled life!

Jesus said, *"I have come that they may have life, and that they may have it more abundantly"* (John 10:10 NKJV).

#2 Your Problem is *Sin*.

What exactly is sin?

Sin is living independently of God's standard—knowing what is right, but choosing what is wrong.

The Bible says, *"If anyone, then, knows the good they ought to do and doesn't do it, it is sin for them"* (James 4:17).

What is the major consequence of sin?

Spiritual death, eternal separation from God.

Scripture states, *"Your iniquities* [sins] *have separated you from your God"* (Isaiah 59:2).

"The wages of sin is death, but the gift of God is eternal life in Christ Jesus our Lord" (Romans 6:23).

#3 God's Provision for You is the *Savior.*

Can anything remove the penalty for sin?

Yes! Jesus died on the cross to personally pay the penalty for your sins.

The Bible says, *"God demonstrates his own love for us in this: While we were still sinners, Christ died for us"* (Romans 5:8).

What is the solution to being separated from God?

Belief in (entrusting your life to) Jesus Christ as the only way to God the Father.

Jesus says, *"I am the way and the truth and the life. No one comes to the Father except through me"* (John 14:6).

"Believe in the Lord Jesus, and you will be saved" (Acts 16:31).

#4 Your Part is *Surrender.*

Give Christ control of your life, entrusting yourself to Him.

"Jesus said to his disciples, 'Whoever wants to be my disciple must deny themselves and take up their cross [die to your own self-rule] *and follow me. For whoever wants to save their life will lose it, but whoever loses their life for me will find it. What good will it be for someone to gain the whole world, yet forfeit their soul?'"* (Matthew 16:24–26).

Place your faith in (rely on) Jesus Christ as your personal Lord and Savior and reject your "good works" as a means of earning God's approval.

"It is by grace you have been saved, through faith—and this is not from yourselves, it is the gift of God—not by works, so that no one can boast" (Ephesians 2:8–9).

The moment you choose to receive Jesus as your Lord and Savior—entrusting your life to Him—He comes to live inside you. Then He gives you His power to live the fulfilled life God has planned for you. If you want to be fully forgiven by God and become the person

God created you to be, you can tell Him in a simple, heartfelt prayer like this:

PRAYER OF SALVATION

*"God, I want a real relationship with You.
I admit that many times I've chosen to
go my own way instead of Your way.
Please forgive me for my sins.
Jesus, thank You for dying on the cross
to pay the penalty for my sins.
Come into my life to be my Lord
and my Savior.
Change me from the inside out
and make me the person
You created me to be.
In Your holy name I pray. Amen."*

WHAT CAN YOU NOW EXPECT?

If you sincerely prayed this prayer, look at what God says!

"I give them eternal life,
and they shall never perish;
no one will snatch them out of my hand.
My Father, who has given them to me,
is greater than all; no one can snatch them
out of my Father's hand.
I and the Father are one."
(John 10:28–30)

STEPS TO SOLUTION

The king considers them the cream of the crop. Of all the young men slated for King Nebuchadnezzar's service, Shadrach, Meshach, and Abednego are most impressive. *"In every matter of wisdom and understanding about which the king questioned them, he found them ten times better than all the magicians and enchanters in his whole kingdom"* (Daniel 1:20).

These exiled Jewish men are committed to serve the Babylonian king with utmost integrity, but soon he issues a decree that violates their allegiance to the one and only true God. The faith of the three men is severely tested, but they manifest a peaceful acceptance of the sovereign hand of God at work.

"The Sovereign LORD has opened my ears;
I have not been rebellious,
I have not turned away. ...
Because the Sovereign LORD helps me,
I will not be disgraced.
Therefore have I set my face like flint,
and I know I will not be put to shame. ...
It is the Sovereign LORD who helps me.
Who will condemn me?
They will all wear out like a garment; the
moths will eat them up."
(Isaiah 50:5, 7, 9)

The king draws a line in the sand! He insists on leading the people both politically and spiritually. Even though the God of Shadrach, Meshach, and Abednego is the only true God, the king creates his own god, a ninety-foot-high by nine-foot-wide image made of gold. After setting it up, a herald proclaims:

"Nations and peoples of every language, this is what you are commanded to do: As soon as you hear the sound of the horn, flute, zither, lyre, harp, pipe and all kinds of music, you must fall down and worship the image of gold that King Nebuchadnezzar has set up. Whoever does not fall down and worship will immediately be thrown into a blazing furnace" (Daniel 3:4–6).

With threats like blazing furnaces, the truth of the following Scripture undergirds their faith.

KEY VERSE TO MEMORIZE

"When you walk through the fire, you will not be burned; the flames will not set you ablaze." (Isaiah 43:2)

Shadrach, Meshach, and Abednego have no intention of complying with the king's edict— their loyalty to the only true God won't let them.

God called them to serve the king and his people, but this direct violation of God's command prompts justified disobedience. These three faithful men are very familiar with the Ten Commandments, including the first two that state *"You shall have no other gods before me"* and *"You shall not make for yourself an* [idol]*"* (Exodus 20:3–4). Therefore obedience to the king's edict is completely out of the question.

This faithful trio serves as examples for us today, not only in obedience to the one true God, but in surrendering to trials that may come as a result of that obedience, surrendering even though it may mean death. Knowing that our true life is hidden with Him and cannot be touched, we can enter into a type of supernatural joy even when facing a fiery furnace. With that knowledge in mind, no matter what the situation, you can *build faith in the furnace.*

Key Passage to Read

Building Faith in the Furnace—James 1:2–12

▶ **FACE** your trial positively.

"Consider it pure joy, my brothers and sisters, whenever you face trials of many kinds" (v. 2).

▶ **PERSEVERE** through your trial patiently.

"Because you know that the testing of your faith produces perseverance" (v. 3).

▶ **FINISH** your trial maturely.

"Let perseverance finish its work so that you may be mature and complete, not lacking anything" (v. 4).

▶ **PRAY** for wisdom consistently.

"If any of you lacks wisdom, you should ask God, who gives generously to all without finding fault, and it will be given to you" (v. 5).

▶ **BELIEVE** in God's answer confidently.

"But when you ask, you must believe and not doubt, because the one who doubts is like a wave of the sea, blown and tossed by the wind. That person should not expect to receive anything from the Lord. Such a person is double-minded and unstable in all they do" (vv. 6–8).

The men sense the blazing furnace awaits; nevertheless, they each persevere.

"Blessed is the one who perseveres under
trial because, having stood the test,
that person will receive the crown of life
that the Lord has promised
to those who love him."
(James 1:12)

Whatever the trial, you can be sure that the eyes of the world are watching carefully, waiting to see how a "Christian" will cope within the crucible of a stressful situation. How will you react? Will you lose faith and curse God? Will the Refiner's fire be too hot to handle? There are always skeptics—those who scrutinize and seek to criticize, the double-minded who doubt and scoff.

It has been said that "Christians may be the only Bible some people read." No doubt in situations of testing, the eyes of the world are on believers! In many ways it could be said that Christians are the only glimpse the outside world has of this Christ we profess to love and serve.

Certainly, God can use trials in our own lives to bring conviction in the hearts of those watching our responses to the refining process.

In the midst of each trial, as we endure the Refiner's fire, let us be mindful of God's divine work in and through our lives—often in ways we may never know this side of heaven—as God demonstrates and authenticates our faith to the watching world.

Scripture reveals a promise for those who persevere ...

> "Come near to God,
> and he will come near to you.
> Wash your hands, you sinners,
> and purify your hearts,
> you double-minded."
> (James 4:8)

Transformation often comes through trials.

Shadrach, Meshach, and Abednego have been "found out." Their disobedience in worshiping the golden image is discovered by a pagan pack—a group of astrologers. The subsequent report to King Nebuchadnezzar: *"There are some Jews whom you have set over the affairs of the province of Babylon—Shadrach, Meshach and Abednego—who pay no attention to you, Your Majesty. They neither serve your gods nor worship the image of gold you have set up"* (Daniel 3:12).

Once considered the cream of the crop, King Nebuchadnezzar now views Shadrach, Meshach, and Abednego as defiant rebels. He is furious by what he perceives as their contemptible act of civil disobedience, and the blazing furnace is foremost on his mind.

The trio of godly men can identify with the following Scriptures ...

"But we have this treasure in jars of clay to show that this all-surpassing power is from God and not from us. We are hard pressed on every side, but not crushed; perplexed, but not in despair; persecuted, but not abandoned; struck down, but not destroyed." (2 Corinthians 4:7–9)

Reaching the Target: Transformation!

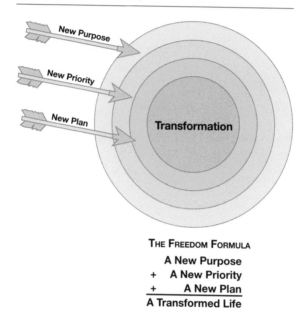

THE FREEDOM FORMULA

A New Purpose
+   A New Priority
+   A New Plan
A Transformed Life

Target #1—A New Purpose: God's purpose for me is to be conformed to the character of Christ.

> *"Those God foreknew he also predestined to be conformed to the image of his Son"* (Romans 8:29).

- "I'll do whatever it takes to be conformed to the character of Christ."

Target #2—A New Priority: God's priority for me is to change my thinking.

> *"Do not conform to the pattern of this world, but be transformed by the renewing of your mind"* (Romans 12:2).

- "I'll do whatever it takes to line up my thinking with God's thinking."

Target #3—A New Plan: God's plan for me is to rely on Christ's strength, not my strength, to be all He created me to be.

> *"I can do all things through him who strengthens me"* (Philippians 4:13 ESV).

- "I'll do whatever it takes to fulfill His plan in His strength."

My Personalized Plan

Through every trial you can experience peace, transformation, and personal growth by depending on the guidelines of God's truth.

▶ **Thankfulness**

- I will thank God for all that He is doing in my life.

> *"Give thanks in all circumstances; for this is God's will for you in Christ Jesus"* (1 Thessalonians 5:18).

▶ Joy

- I will rejoice in the Lord, knowing that the outcome of every trial is in His hands.

"We rejoice in our sufferings, knowing that suffering produces endurance" (Romans 5:3 ESV).

▶ Confession

- I will ask God to search my heart, and I will confess any hidden sin.

"Whoever conceals their sins does not prosper, but the one who confesses and renounces them finds mercy" (Proverbs 28:13).

▶ Humility

- I will remember that God gives grace to the brokenhearted.

"He gives us more grace. That is why Scripture says: 'God opposes the proud but shows favor to the humble'" (James 4:6).

▶ Obedience

- I will learn to hear and obey God's voice.

"This is love: that we walk in obedience to his commands. As you have heard from the beginning, his command is that you walk in love" (2 John 6).

▶ Wisdom

- I will saturate my mind with Scripture.

"I meditate on your precepts and consider your ways. I delight in your decrees; I will not neglect your word" (Psalm 119:15–16).

▶ Prayer

- I will not worry, but pray about everything.

"Do not be anxious about anything, but in every situation, by prayer and petition, with thanksgiving, present your requests to God. And the peace of God, which transcends all understanding, will guard your hearts and your minds in Christ Jesus" (Philippians 4:6–7).

▶ Trust

- I will entrust myself to God, who judges justly.

"When they hurled their insults at him, he did not retaliate; when he suffered, he made no threats. Instead, he entrusted himself to him who judges justly" (1 Peter 2:23).

▶ Dependence

- I will act in the power of Christ.

"I can do all this through Christ who strengthens me" (Philippians 4:13 NKJV).

▶ Endurance

- I will look to the Lord for deliverance.

"No temptation has seized you except what is common to mankind. And God is faithful; he will not let you be tempted beyond what you can bear. But when you are tempted, he will also provide a way out so that you can endure it" (1 Corinthians 10:13).

▶ Praise

- I will focus on God's greatness, not on my circumstances.

"Through Jesus, therefore, let us continually offer to God a sacrifice of praise—the fruit of lips that openly profess his name" (Hebrews 13:15).

▶ Ministry

- I will look for ways to reach out and help others.

"Praise be to the God and Father of our Lord Jesus Christ, the Father of compassion and the God of all comfort, who comforts us in all our troubles, so that we can comfort those in any trouble with the comfort we ourselves receive from God" (2 Corinthians 1:3–4).

Despite the anticipation of feeling the heat steady resolve prevails and faith flourishes.

There are no desperate pleas or petitions from Shadrach, Meshach, and Abednego. There is no groveling before King Nebuchadnezzar to rescind his life-or-death edict. There is simply a declaration of faith in tribute to their God, the one and only true God.

"If we are thrown into the blazing furnace, the God we serve is able to deliver us from it, and he will deliver us from Your Majesty's hand. But even if he does not, we want you to know, Your Majesty, that we will not serve your gods or worship the image of gold you have set up" (Daniel 3:17–18).

Shadrach, Meshach, and Abednego can be counted among the purified in the following Scripture...

"Many will be purified,
made spotless and refined,
but the wicked will continue to be wicked.
None of the wicked will understand,
but those who are wise will understand."
(Daniel 12:10)

Stepping into a blazing fiery furnace and then staying there is beyond the comprehension of most of us. It would take just a word of praise, only a bending of the knee and the flames could be avoided. But the three young men would not sell their God short nor trade eternity for more time here.

When you are facing a fiery furnace, there are things you need to know about God's relationship with you that will strengthen your resolve and keep you in the fire until it has done its work in your heart.

KNOW THAT ...

▶**God loves you.**

"For I am convinced that neither death nor life, neither angels nor demons, neither the present nor the future, nor any powers, neither height nor depth, nor anything else in all creation, will be able to separate us from the love of God that is in Christ Jesus our Lord" (Romans 8:38–39).

▶**God is with you.**

"Never will I leave you; never will I forsake you" (Hebrews 13:5).

▶**God cares** about your struggle.

"Cast all your anxiety on him because he cares for you" (1 Peter 5:7).

▶ **God understands** your weaknesses.

"For we do not have a high priest who is unable to empathize with our weaknesses, but we have one who has been tempted in every way, just as we are—yet he did not sin" (Hebrews 4:15).

▶ **God controls** your circumstances.

"Praise be to the name of God for ever and ever; wisdom and power are his. He changes times and seasons; he deposes kings and raises up others. He gives wisdom to the wise and knowledge to the discerning. He reveals deep and hidden things; he knows what lies in darkness, and light dwells with him. I thank and praise you, God of my ancestors: You have given me wisdom and power, you have made known to me what we asked of you, you have made known to us the dream of the king" (Daniel 2:20–23).

▶ **God increases** your compassion.

"Praise be to the God and Father of our Lord Jesus Christ, the Father of compassion and the God of all comfort, who comforts us in all our troubles, so that we can comfort those in any trouble with the comfort we ourselves receive from God" (2 Corinthians 1:3–4).

▶ **God is trustworthy.**

"Oh, the depth of the riches of the wisdom and knowledge of God! How unsearchable his judgments, and his paths beyond tracing out!" (Romans 11:33).

▶ **God increases** your expectations.

"Now to him who is able to do immeasurably more than all we ask or imagine, according to his power that is at work within us, to him be glory in the church and in Christ Jesus throughout all generations, for ever and ever! Amen" (Ephesians 3:20–21).

▶ **God redeems** your mistakes.

"[He] gave himself for us to redeem us from all wickedness and to purify for himself a people that are his very own, eager to do what is good" (Titus 2:14).

▶ **God gives** sufficient grace.

"You then, my son, be strong in the grace that is in Christ Jesus" (2 Timothy 2:1).

▶ **God has your future** in His hands.

"Forget the former things; do not dwell on the past. See, I am doing a new thing! Now it springs up; do you not perceive it? I am making a way in the wilderness and streams in the wasteland" (Isaiah 43:18–19).

Jesus said …

"In this world you will have trouble. But take heart! I have overcome the world."
(John 16:33)

HOW TO Tell Yourself the Truth

King Nebuchadnezzar wants nothing to do with the truth. He isn't moved in the least bit by Shadrach, Meshach, and Abednego's diehard devotion to their God.

He remains enraged and issues an even more deadly directive—turn up the furnace seven times hotter.

The king then orders some of his strongest soldiers to tie up the three men and throw them into the furnace, but following the king's commands proves fatal. The soldiers die from the furnace's lapping flames. Shadrach, Meshach, and Abednego are now fully engulfed, however, and presumed dead on the floor of the fiery furnace. But suddenly King Nebuchadnezzar sees something that makes him leap to his feet in amazement and stirs his heart toward the God of Shadrach, Meshach, and Abednego.

"Look! I see four men walking around in the fire, unbound and unharmed, and the fourth looks like a son of the gods" (Daniel 3:25).

Then the king approached the furnace and declared, *"Shadrach, Meshach, and Abednego, servants of the Most High God, come out! Come here!"*

They walked out and were completely unscathed, without even a trace of smoke.

Either an angel or a preincarnate appearance of Jesus delivers the three men of God from their fiery trial, prompting King Nebuchadnezzar to proclaim ...

"Praise be to the God of Shadrach, Meshach and Abednego, who has sent his angel and rescued his servants! They trusted in him and defied the king's command and were willing to give up their lives rather than serve or worship any god except their own God. Therefore I decree that the people of any nation or language who say anything against the God of Shadrach, Meshach and Abednego be cut into pieces and their houses be turned into piles of rubble, for no other god can save in this way." (Daniel 3:28–29)

Just as you need to enter a trial knowing some things about God's relationship to you, it is also important to keep in mind some critical facts regarding your relationship to Him.

KNOW with certainty that your life is surrendered to the Lord Jesus Christ.

▶**TELL YOURSELF**

"I am a child of God!"

TRUTH

"See what great love the Father has lavished on us, that we should be called children of God! And that is what we are!" (1 John 3:1).

KNOW that your unsaved self (the "old" you who was enslaved to sin) was crucified with Christ.

▶**TELL YOURSELF**

"I am dead to sinful ways!"

TRUTH

"For we know that our old self was crucified with him so that the body ruled by sin might be done away with, that we should no longer be slaves to sin" (Romans 6:6).

KNOW that you have been separated from the power of sin.

▶ **TELL YOURSELF**

"I may want to sin, but I don't have to!"

TRUTH

"Do not let sin reign in your mortal body so that you obey its evil desires" (Romans 6:12).

KNOW that sin need not control you.

▶ **TELL YOURSELF**

"When I respond in a sinful way, I am making a choice!"

TRUTH

"Sin shall no longer be your master, because you are not under law, but under grace" (Romans 6:14).

KNOW that there is power in God's Word. Commit Romans 6:1–2 to memory and quote it when you are tempted to sin.

▶ **TELL YOURSELF**

"I will not continue to sin!"

TRUTH

"What shall we say, then? Shall we go on sinning so that grace may increase? By no

means! We are those who have died to sin; how can we live in it any longer?" (Romans 6:1–2).

KNOW that the Spirit of Christ lives in you.

▶TELL YOURSELF

"I have the power of Christ in me!"

TRUTH

"If Christ is in you, then even though your body is subject to death because of sin, the Spirit gives life because of righteousness. And if the Spirit of him who raised Jesus from the dead is living in you, he who raised Christ from the dead will also give life to your mortal bodies because of his Spirit who lives in you" (Romans 8:10–11).

KNOW that you can face trials from a position of victory.

▶TELL YOURSELF

"My battle has already been won!"

TRUTH

"God raised us up with Christ and seated us with him in the heavenly realms in Christ Jesus" (Ephesians 2:6).

KNOW that you are an instrument of righteousness for God.

▶ TELL YOURSELF

"I will give God total authority over everything I do and say!"

TRUTH

"Do not offer any part of yourself to sin as an instrument of wickedness, but rather offer yourselves to God as those who have been brought from death to life; and offer every part of yourself to him as an instrument of righteousness" (Romans 6:13).

KNOW that you live in the presence of Christ.

▶ TELL YOURSELF

"I willingly submit to the convicting direction and guidance of the Holy Spirit!"

TRUTH

"So I say, walk by the Spirit, and you will not gratify the desires of the flesh. ... Since we live by the Spirit, let us keep in step with the Spirit" (Galatians 5:16, 25).

KNOW **that you are God's child.**

▶ **TELL YOURSELF**

"I am God's child. I am led by His Spirit."

TRUTH

"For if [I] *live according to the flesh,* [I] *will die; but if by the Spirit* [I] *put to death the misdeeds of the body,* [I] *will live. For those who are led by the Spirit of God are the children of God"* (Romans 8:13–14).

HOW TO Accept the Sovereignty of God

The word *sovereignty* means "supreme power" and "freedom from external control."[6] These definitions describe God perfectly because no higher power exists, and He is certainly free from other controlling influences.

The Bible says ...

> "He changes times and seasons;
> he sets up kings and deposes them;
> he gives wisdom to the wise
> and knowledge to the discerning."
> (Daniel 2:21)

Ten Steps to Accepting God's Sovereignty

1 Seek God in prayer for discernment in your circumstances.

"Lord God, how I need Your wisdom, Your discernment, Your understanding."

"Is any one of you in trouble? He should pray" (James 5:13).

2 Open your heart to God with complete honesty about your feelings.

"I am so confused—my emotions go up one minute, down the next."

"Cast your cares on the LORD and he will sustain you; he will never let the righteous fall" (Psalm 55:22).

3 Verify your belief in God's love for you.

"Thank You that You love me, no matter what."

"Though he brings grief, he will show compassion, so great is his unfailing love" (Lamentations 3:32).

4 **Expect God to change your life through the truth He reveals to you.**

"Thank You that through this trial, You will teach me and change me."

"It was good for me to be afflicted so that I might learn your decrees" (Psalm 119:71).

5 **Realize that God is all-powerful and sovereign over your circumstances.**

"I realize that all power is in Your hands."

Pilate said, *"Don't you realize I have power either to free you or to crucify you?"* (John 19:10)

Jesus answered, *"You would have no power over me if it were not given to you from above"* (John 19:11).

6 **Trust God to work through all things to prove your faith and to bring Him praise, glory, and honor.**

"I realize that You will use all situations, even bad ones, to strengthen my faith and to glorify Yourself."

"The God of all grace, who called you to his eternal glory in Christ, after you have suffered a little while, will himself restore

you and make you strong, firm and steadfast" (1 Peter 5:10).

7 **Invest time in studying Scripture and in prayer.**

"I want to immerse myself in Your Word and in Your truths."

"I meditate on your precepts and consider your ways. I delight in your decrees; I will not neglect your word" (Psalm 119:15–16).

8 **Gain an eternal perspective of God's purposes for your present pain.**

"I want to see beyond this situation to Your purpose for it."

"'Neither this man nor his parents sinned,' said Jesus, 'but this happened so that the work of God might be displayed in his life'" (John 9:3).

9 **Turn to the indwelling Christ, who provides you with His power for victory.**

"Thank You that I can rely on Christ within me to live His life through me."

"I can do everything through him who gives me strength" (Philippians 4:13).

10 Yield to God's sovereignty. You may never understand or have any answers for your suffering.

"I don't have to have all the answers, but I can know the God who does. I yield myself to Your sovereign control."

"Trust in the LORD with all your heart
and lean not on your own understanding;
in all your ways acknowledge him,
and he will make your paths straight."
(Proverbs 3:5–6)

HOW TO Pray to the God of All Comfort

Scripture provides healing salve in the midst of sorrow, sadness, and the painful trials of life. As we open the Bible, one verse leads to another while we read personal accounts of God's tender comfort during times of deeper trials and tribulations.

What an encouragement to know that our faithful God is the same yesterday, today, and forever, and in His love He is continually offering comfort as only He can.

The instructions in Scripture are simple and effective. These three instructions from the Word of God apply to any and all trials ...

"Be joyful in hope, patient in affliction, faithful in prayer."
(Romans 12:12)

When you are in need of comfort during a trial, pray this prayer to the God of all comfort ...

"Lord, I look to You as my Comforter in this great sorrow!
Even though I'm walking through this valley of darkness,
I choose to not live in fear,
for You are with me!
You comfort me.
Just as a parent who comforts a child,
You are the One who comforts me.
Your promise of unfailing love provides comfort to my spirit.
Even though You make me face many troubles and heartaches,
You always bring me through them, restoring my peace once more.
When I grieve over my trials and heartaches, I know I'm blessed because I grow closer to You!
In Your precious name I pray. Amen"

"You who are my Comforter in sorrow, my heart is faint within me."
(Jeremiah 8:18)

HOW FIRM A FOUNDATION, 1787

(Stanza 3)

*"When thro' fiery trials
your pathway shall lie,
My grace, all-sufficient
shall be your supply;
The flame shall not hurt you;
I only design Your dross to consume,
and Your gold to refine."*[7]

SCRIPTURES TO MEMORIZE

Does God promise to **be with** me when life seems to hand me more than I can bear, when my pain is so unbearable that I fear it will **sweep** over me, drowning me in despair?

"When you pass through the waters, I will ***be with*** *you; and when you pass through the rivers, they will not* ***sweep*** *over you. When you walk through the fire, you will not be burned; the flames will not set you ablaze."* (Isaiah 43:2)

Can God use something as objectionable as **suffering** to **produce hope**?

"We also glory in our sufferings, because we know that ***suffering produces*** *perseverance; perseverance, character; and character,* ***hope****."* (Romans 5:3–4)

Do all Christians experience **trials** that will **test** them in this sinful world?

"Beloved, do not be surprised at the fiery ***trial*** *when it comes upon you to* ***test*** *you, as though something strange were happening to you. But rejoice insofar as you share Christ's sufferings, that you may also rejoice and be glad when his glory is revealed."* (1 Peter 4:12–13 ESV)

Am I to **rejoice** when I **suffer grief in all kinds of trials**? Can my suffering **result in praise, glory, and honor**?

*"In this you greatly **rejoice**, though now for a little while you may have had to **suffer grief in all kinds of trials**. These have come so that the proven genuineness of your faith— of greater worth than gold, which perishes even though refined by fire— may **result in praise, glory and honor** when Jesus Christ is revealed."* (1 Peter 1:6–7)

How am I to respond when **weaknesses, hardships**, and **difficulties** come my way? Will these actually help me to become a **strong** person?

*"That is why, for Christ's sake, I delight in **weaknesses**, in insults, in **hardships**, in persecutions, in **difficulties**. For when I am weak, then I am **strong**."* (2 Corinthians 12:10)

Even though **discipline** is **painful**, can it still **produce righteousness and peace for those who have been trained by it**?

*"No **discipline** seems pleasant at the time, but **painful**. Later on, however, it **produces a harvest of righteousness and peace for those who have been trained by it**."* (Hebrews 12:11)

Does God **rescue godly** people **from** their **trials?** Will He hold **unrighteous** people accountable with **judgment** and **punishment?**

*"The Lord knows how to **rescue** the **godly from trials** and to hold the **unrighteous** for **punishment** on the day of **judgment.**"* (2 Peter 2:9)

Can I expect **God** to **work all things for** my **good?** Am I **predestined to be conformed to the image of His Son**, Jesus Christ?

*"We know that in **all things God works for** the **good** of those who love him, who have been called according to his purpose. For those God foreknew he also **predestined to be conformed to the image of his Son.**"* (Romans 8:28–29)

Am I to experience **joy** when I **face trials?** Will the **testing of** my **faith produce perseverance** and help to make me **mature** and **complete** in the Lord?

*"Consider it pure **joy,** my brothers and sisters, whenever you **face trials** of many kinds, because you know that the **testing of** your **faith produces perseverance.** Let perseverance finish its work so that you may be **mature** and **complete,** not lacking anything."* (James 1:2–4)

NOTES

1. *Merriam-Webster Collegiate Dictionary* (2001); available from http://www.m-w.com.

2. *Merriam-Webster Collegiate Dictionary.*

3. W. E. Vine, *Vine's Complete Expository Dictionary of Biblical Words*, electronic ed. (Nashville: Thomas Nelson, 1996).

4. http://info.goldavenue.com/info_site/in_glos/in_glos_wolhill.html.

5. Lawrence J. Crabb, Jr., *Understanding People: Deep Longings for Relationship*, Ministry Resources Library (Grand Rapids: Zondervan, 1987), 15–16; Robert S. McGee, *The Search for Significance*, 2nd ed. (Houston, TX: Rapha, 1990), 27–30.

6. *Merriam-Webster Collegiate Dictionary*, s.v. "Sovereignty."

7. *Logos Hymnal.* 1st edition, Oak Harbor, WA: Logos Research Systems, Inc., 1995.

HOPE FOR THE HEART TITLES